# WILD ABOUT CHILI

## BY DOTTY GRIFFITH

**BARRON'S**

New York • London • Toronto • Sydney

For recipe acknowledgments, see page 104.

*All inquiries should be addressed to:*
Barron's Educational Series, Inc.
250 Wireless Boulevard
Hauppauge, N.Y. 11788

Library of Congress No. 85-3974
International Standard Book No. 0-8120-3498-8

**Library of Congress Cataloging in Publication Data**
Griffith, Dotty.
 Wild about chili.

 Includes index.
 1. Chili con carne.   I. Title.
TX749.G83   1985        641.8'23        85-3974
ISBN 0-8120-3498-8

Design by Milton Glaser, Inc.
Color photographs by Karen Leeds
Helga Weinrib, food stylist
Linda Peacock, prop stylist

Shawls in Chili Tostada Stack, 3-Way Cincinnati Chili,
and Chili Hash Browns all courtesy of Runa Maki
Imports.

PRINTED IN HONG KONG

0 1 2 3    4 9 0    9 8 7 6 5 4 3

# CONTENTS

# INTRODUCTION

C hili was born a peasant food, a simple but highly spiced meat stew. Ah, but it has grown up to be so much more.

It is a food that excites even the most mild-mannered of persons, many of whom might otherwise not be cooks. Just as football fanatics believe they can call plays better than the coach of the moment, so do chili aficionados devoutly believe that their recipe is superior to anyone else's.

That conviction has spawned a national pastime: the chili cook-off. From one end of this country to the other on just about any weekend, chili cooks pit their best (and often secret) recipes against those of other cooks, usually for nothing more than a trophy and the thrill of victory.

They travel in recreational vehicles, pickup trucks, or just about anything else that will get them to the cook-offs, some of which are held in remote ghost towns or rugged mountain areas. They wage a variation of mano a mano combat: "spoon to spoon" confrontation.

Chili is, after all, a very macho food. Of course, there are many women who are excellent chili cooks. But regardless of who cooks it, chili is not for a ladies' tea. It is most often eaten before, during, and after sporting events or on cold, wintry evenings that test the mettle of man and beast.

Besides being a national pastime, chili is an individual passion. In recent years, chili cooks haven't been content to argue about whose chili is best; they've even squabbled about which cook-off is the real championship event. But more on extremes of chili hubris later.

What exactly is this dish that generates such heat and emotion? Its most correct name is chili con carne, *Spanish words that literally mean "chile peppers with meat." Granted, it might make sense if the name were* carne con chile, *but that's too late to change now. Whenever you say* chili *or* chili con carne, *most folks know you're talking about a highly spiced stew. In this book,* chili *refers to the dish itself, while* chile *or* chiles *refer to the fresh or dried peppers with which the savory stew is seasoned.*

That sounds simple enough. But anyone who thinks chili is chili is chili doesn't know beans about chili.

And speaking of beans ... let's get this straight. Beans have their place, but it is not in chili—at least in authentic Texas chili. Beans quite appropriately may be cooked on the stove next to chili and served on the side with chili, in case the connoisseur opts to mix the two. But cooking chili with beans in the same pot is a touch of heresy, even though it has gained widespread acceptance in many corners. Therefore, in this book, you will find a few recipes *for chili with beans and even one for chili with beans and no meat.*

*The "bean issue" serves to underscore the point that one person's chili is another's stew or meat sauce. In the eyes of this native Texan, chili is not just a macho food, it's a very personal one. What I consider "real" chili may not meet your expectations at all. But that's why this book offers a broad range of chili recipes.*

*If any further evidence of the individuality of chili is necessary, I offer this anecdote. When my husband, Tom Stephenson, first moved to Dallas more than ten years ago to work for* The Dallas Morning News, *several of us on the night reporting staff convened at my apartment for a midnight "bowl of red." He, being the only non-Texan in the group, coughed and gasped upon his first spoonful. Finally, he sputtered, "Is this a cruel joke?" A native of Kansas City, Mo., he was used to a much milder concoction and couldn't quite believe that some of us could consume more hot chili than cold beer at one sitting.*

*Now a restaurateur, Tom has come a long way since then, and his establishments serve a much hotter version than my original recipe. During the writing of this book, he tasted most of the recipes, and to his present palate, hotter usually means better. Likewise, our five-year-old son, Kelly, one of the most dedicated of chili-tasters, turned thumbs down on those recipes he felt weren't hot enough. His palate has been trained on spicy foods, from chili to Tex-Mex to barbecue.*

*Let me hasten to add, however, that hot or not, any good chili must have a pleasing harmony of flavors. You will find a wide range of hotness in the chilis in this book. Chili that simply clears your sinuses is not great nor even good chili. It must tickle the tastebuds and leave a pleasant aftertaste. Much like wine, its bouquet must be inviting. And like wine, it comes in a variety of styles, flavors, colors, and consistencies. The judges at chili cook-offs, like wine-tasters, evaluate the competition on color, aroma, consistency, taste, and aftertaste.*

*Techniques for cooking chili are almost as varied as the intensity, taste, and seasonings. Most commonly, recipes call for searing the meat, adding spices and liquid, then simmering the stew until the meat is tender. But as the recipes in this book reveal, there are several ways to cook chili.*

*In spite of the variations, most of the techniques are very simple. That's because chili is, after all, fare for common folk. Chili most probably originated in the modest kitchens of mid nineteenth-century Texans, according to Frank X. Tolbert, a* Dallas Morning News *columnist for many years and the world's greatest authority on chili at the time of his death in 1984.*

*In his book,* A Bowl of Red *(first published in 1953, last revised in 1983), Tolbert speculated that chili first was cooked in San Antonio. That is a likely place for its birth, since San Antonio best represents the mix of cultures that was early Texas—Spanish, Mexican, American and European. Although often considered Mexican, chili is in fact Texan. It is not a food found in Mexico, although the influence of Mexican cuisine is undeniable.*

*Its ancestry has been a source of much speculation, according to Bill Bridges, author of* The Great American Chili Book. *One theory gives credit to a group of Canary Islands immigrants who brought cumin to Texas in 1731. Chili was born, according to the story, when the islanders put their favorite spice to a primitive mixture of meat and ground chile peppers already cooked by San Antonio settlers. The addition is so important because cumin is what gives the dish its enchanting aroma.*

*Other historians, according to Bridges, believe chili evolved from a mixture of dried meat and spices, similar to the Indians' pemmican, that was eaten on the trail by soldiers and cowboys. Later, washerwomen, or* lavanderas, *followed armies around Texas doing their laundry and preparing hot meals. They apparently were better known for their cooking, particularly a stew of beef, venison, or goat seasoned with native wild marjoram and red chile.*

*Known as "son-of-a-bitch stew," this concoction, according to this theory, was the forerunner of chili.*

*Regardless of how it began, chili first came out of the kitchens and onto the streets of San Antonio in the 1880s, according to Tolbert's book. So-called chili queens made their chili in big pots, then toted them around town on crudely made carts. Wherever they felt hungry traffic would pass, they set up their "takeout shops," building small mesquite or charcoal fires to keep the pots warm while they peddled their fiery wares.*

*In this chapter in chili history, the dish became truly egalitarian, because the common man and the aristocrat alike could not resist the piquant aroma. With the advent of chili powder in the 1890s, chili spread to cafes and homes all over the state and beyond.*

*It is not known for certain who developed chili powder, but two names are almost always mentioned in discussions: William Gebhardt, of New Braunfels, Texas, who founded the canned chili company that bore his name; and DeWitt Clinton Pendery, a grocer from Fort Worth.*

*Generally, Gebhardt gets the credit for the invention of chili powder, although even the company spokesman can't verify it. Because Gebhardt left his business soon after launching it, there is precious little information about the*

*man. According to Tolbert, this is what's known: In 1896,
Gebhardt invented a machine that ground chili powder
from dried ancho pods. That same year, he brought it from
New Braunfels to San Antonio, where he canned the first
commercial chili in 1908.*

*Tolbert also presents a good case for Clinton. As early
as the 1880s, the grocer noted that many of his customers
asked for chile peppers and spices for making chili con
carne. In 1890—six years before Gebhardt's invention—he
began advertising a blend of chili powder and other
seasonings for making the dish.*

*No matter who developed the powder, it made short
work of the previously arduous task of hand-grinding the
dried chile peppers. And the powder made chili as close to
a convenience food as there was around the turn of the
century.*

*Considering its humble beginnings, chili recipes
traditionally have used cheaper, less tender, and sometimes
greasy cuts of beef. What supermarkets often sell as "chili
meat" is coarsely ground hamburger meat that's about 65
to 70 percent lean. But chili can be made with a variety of
beef cuts, from round steak to chuck roast. (Some cuts,
however, can be too tender for chili. Sirloin, for instance,
tends to break down too much during cooking.)*

*Generally, the leaner the meat, the better the chili. A
small amount of fat or oil can be added for flavor, but*

*some championship cooks are now leaving out any additional fat.*

*Of course, chili can be made with many other meats, alone or in combination with beef. In this book, you'll find recipes for chili with pork, venison, and chicken.*

*Whether the original chili queens took as much pride and care in preparation of the dish as modern chili gladiators is unknown. Today, there are several schools of chili preparation. Some cooks, for example, subscribe to the braising method, others to the stewing method. Some use chili powder, others use pure ground peppers. Some season before stewing to allow the flavors to cook in and meld; others season toward the end of cooking for the strongest, freshest flavor.*

*In recent years, prize-winning chili cooks have favored stewing the meat—cooking in liquid without first searing. This reduces the total cooking time and prevents the meat from getting too soft. Prize-winners also have tended toward seasoning later. Generally, the meat is cooked until tender, then seasoned and cooked only a brief while longer.*

*Traditionally, chili is thickened with masa, the meal used for corn tortillas, but prize-winners now lean more toward no additional thickening, and instead simmer the stew to the perfect consistency. When thickening is needed, many rely on additional chili powder.*

*The most authentic way to season chili is to use fresh and dried chile peppers instead of chili powder. This, of course, is considerably more trouble. The dried chiles must first be softened in water, then puréed, along with any fresh ones, with some liquid, water, or tomatoes.*

*You may have heard that tomatoes are as forbidden in chili as beans. Not so. Puréed tomatoes do a lot to add color and consistency to many good chilis. The trick is to render them a silent partner in the recipe.*

*Although chili cook-offs take place virtually year-round, the three major championships are held every fall. Each one claims to crown the best chili cook under the sun.*

*Every October, the International Chili Society (ICS) holds the "world championship," a title the group holds legal rights to use. Then on the first Saturday in November, West Texas' Big Bend country comes alive when Terlingua, a virtual ghost town with twenty-five inhabitants, welcomes participants and spectators back to the spawning ground of the cook-off phenomenon.*

*Chili cook-offs date back to 1967 when Frank X. Tolbert and a group of his friends came up with the idea of staging a competition to promote his recently revised book,* A Bowl of Red. *Public relations executives Tom Tierny and Bill Neale, race-car driver Carroll Shelby, and attorney David Witts were all present at the original cook-*

*off, which pitted New York humorist H. Allen Smith and Texas newspaperman Wick Fowler.*

*Previously, Tolbert had dueled in print with Smith about what constituted "real chili." Fowler, as chief cook of the ephemeral Chili Appreciation Society International (CASI), was selected as the one to defend the honor of an authentic bowl of red. Smith's recipe contained green bell peppers and kidney beans; Fowler's was a pristine concoction of meat and spices. Despite the sharp contrast, the first CASI contest ended in a draw.*

*Since those days, the world of cook-offs has gotten quite a bit more complicated. In 1975, a group of California "chiliheads" led by C. V. Wood Jr., an associate of Shelby, clashed with Tolbert and began a rival cook-off near Los Angeles under the auspices of the ICS. Meanwhile, the cook-off in Terlingua continued under the guidance of Tolbert and CASI.*

*In the following years, much ado was made in newspaper columns (most authored by Tolbert) about the "copycat California cook-off." While the war was real, it also helped to promote interest in both events.*

*Chili cooks competed year 'round in cook-offs, sanctioned either by ICS or CASI, to earn the right to qualify for one of the championship cook-offs.*

*Then, in 1983, yet another schism divided the cook-off world when CASI and Tolbert parted ways. Both held cook-*

*offs on the same day in Terlingua. Both purported to be the championship. Despite Tolbert's death, the chili duel in Terlingua continued in 1984, and both sides showed no real desire to mend the rift.*

*The CASI cook-off is officially known as the CASI Terlingua Chili Championship. The one Tolbert founded in 1983 is called the Original Terlingua International Frank X. Tolbert–Wick Fowler Memorial Championship Chili Cook-Off.*

*Whether the chili world will ever unite remains to be seen. Until then, chili aficionados can keep up with each camp's goings-on by reading chili publications. The "Official Publication of the International Chili Society" is available by writing P.O. Box 2966, Dept. A, Newport Beach, California 92663. CASI cook-offs and other Texas-related chili happenings are chronicled in "Chili Monthly"; mailing address is P.O. Box 189, Martindale, Texas 78655 and in the "Goat Gap Gazette"; 5110 Bayard Lane No. 2, Houston, Texas 77006.*

*This book is all about chili. About half the recipes are devoted to the making of chili; the remainder are recipes that incorporate chili. Some are based on traditional Mexican or Tex-Mex tastes; others show you how to use chili in ways you probably never have considered. But once you get started, you'll be wild about chili.*

# CONVERSION TABLES

*The weights and measures used in the list of ingredients and cooking instructions for each recipe are given in both the customary U.S. measurements and in metric measures. When following the recipes, use the measurement you are most comfortable with, and do not mix metric measures with U.S. measures.*

## FOR BRITISH AND AUSTRALIAN COOKS

*British and Australian cooks measure many more items by weight than do Americans, who prefer cup measures for items such as rice, flour, chopped peppers, and so on. Here are some approximate equivalents for basic items used in this book. (So as to avoid awkward measurements, some conversions are rounded off to the nearest equivalent measure.)*

|  | U.S. Customary | Imperial |
|---|---|---|
| Butter | 1 tablespoon | ½ ounce |
|  | ¼ cup | 2 ounces |
|  | ½ cup | 4 ounces |
|  | 1 cup | 8 ounces |
| Flour, all-purpose (plain), sifted | ¼ cup | 1¼ ounces |
|  | ½ cup | 2½ ounces |
|  | 1 cup | 5 ounces |

| | U.S. Customary | Imperial |
|---|---|---|
| Flour, all-purpose (plain), sifted (con't) | 1½ cups | 1½ ounces |
| | 2 cups | 10 ounces |
| Grated cheese | ½ cup | 2 ounces |
| | 1 cup | 4 ounces |
| Chopped vegetables | ½ cup | 2 ounces |
| | 1 cup | 4 ounces |
| Rice (uncooked) | 1 cup | 8 ounces |

## LIQUID MEASURES

*The Imperial cup used to measure liquid ingredients is considerably larger than the U.S. cup. Use the following table to convert liquid measurements to Imperial units, and be especially careful when doubling recipes.*

| AMERICAN CUP (in book) | IMPERIAL CUP (adjusts to) |
|---|---|
| ¼ cup | 4 tablespoons |
| ⅓ cup | 5 tablespoons |
| 1 cup | ¼ pint + 6 tablespoons |
| 1½ cups | ½ pint + 4 tablespoons |
| 2 cups | ¾ pint |
| 3 cups | 1½ pints |
| 5 cups | 2 pints |

*Note:* The Australian and Canadian cup measures 250 ml and is only slightly larger than the U.S. cup, which is 236 ml. Cooks in Australia and Canada can follow the exact measurements given in the recipes, using either the U.S. or metric measures.

# OVEN TEMPERATURES

*British cooks should use the following settings:*

| Gas Mark | ¼ | 2 | 4 | 6 | 8 |
|---|---|---|---|---|---|
| Fahrenheit | 225 | 300 | 350 | 400 | 450 |
| Celsius | 110 | 150 | 180 | 200 | 230 |

# COOKING TECHNIQUES

N ow that you've been introduced to chili, let's get
down to the business of cooking it.
As already mentioned, there are several techniques.
Some take longer than others; some work better with
less tender cuts; some are even developed primarily for
competition. In fact, a number of chili cooks swear that
what they submit to cook-off judges isn't something they
would like to eat at home when they're making chili for
eating enjoyment.

The most traditional way to prepare chili is to sear the
meat (usually in a small amount of fat), add the spices
and liquid, simmer until the meat is tender, and thicken
the stew near the end of cooking time. This approach is the
best on a lazy, winter day when you have time to enjoy the
aroma of chili wafting from the kitchen. It also allows the
use of less tender, economical cuts. (Because good chili
contains so much meat, it is not necessarily an inexpensive
dish, in spite of its peasant origins.)

With this method, the spices are allowed to permeate
the meat and mellow the stew, so there is less likely to be
an afterburn to the tongue or digestive tract. Often, it is
desirable to cook chili in this fashion, let it cool, then
refrigerate it overnight to give the flavors still more time to

meld. This also gives the cook a chance to remove any excess fat from the stew; the grease will congeal at the top, and can be easily skimmed off.

Of late, championship chili cooks have revised the traditional cooking process, primarily by eliminating thickening agents and extra fat and by adding some or all of the spices near the end of the cooking. Adding spices at the end gives an intense flavor; and competitive cooks have adopted this technique so their chili will make an impression on the judges. Sometimes, however, it can make too much of an impression. If added too near the end, the result can be a harsh, almost raw taste.

Why the deviation? At most cook-offs, judges are served the chili in the small styrofoam cups most often used for take-out coffee. By the time the spoon reaches the mouth, however, the chili may have cooled, and thus lost some of its intense flavor. This occurs most frequently at the large cook-offs, where a chili may have to go through preliminary judging before advancing to the finals—a procedure that may take an hour or more. Some cooks also feel that the styrofoam containers actually absorb some of the chili's flavor. Often, they dust the inside of their judging cups with chili powder to "seal" the styrofoam.

This book explores all these cooking methods. While most recipes rely on the traditional techniques, some, especially those from championship chili cooks, apply some of the variations on the time-honored chili theme.

*Just as there are different cooking methods, there are different ways to season chili as well. Certainly chili powder is the most often used basic ingredient. After all, the invention of chili powder made chili easily accessible to the home cook, but some of the most savory concoctions can be made by using a combination of fresh and dried chiles, with or without the addition of chili powder.*

*Although this technique is considerably more trouble, the results can be quite gratifying. Two recipes that use this technique are Favorite Chili and Deep Hole Chili, and another, Homestyle Chili, uses an adaptation.*

*While chili recipes often call for adding a bit of fat or oil for browning the meat, many cooks prefer to leave out the additional fat, particularly in competition, again because of the lengthy judging. By the time the chili gets to the finals, the fat may have already risen to the top and started to congeal—a turnoff to most any judge. But health concerns have also encouraged many chili cooks to omit the traditional touch of suet.*

*To make chili with a minimum of fat, many cooks sear the meats in pots with nonstick surfaces instead of the traditional cast-iron pots. Other cooks eliminate the searing step altogether. This also can make the meat look more red because there is absolutely no browning. This book includes recipes with and without added fat.*

*The thickening agent used in chili traditionally has*
*been cornmeal or masa harina (a corn flour usually used*

for making tortillas). The addition of either ingredient adds a distinctive flavor to chili, but it also presents certain problems. The thickener can just as easily lump up or add a raw grain taste that might soften the flavor of the chili. That is why some competitive cooks prefer to thicken their chilis by just cooking them down. A number also may add more chili powder to achieve a hearty consistency.

Some recipes in this book call for thickening with masa trigo, a wheat-flour mixture used in making flour tortillas. It consists of wheat flour, lard, leavening, and salt, and it seems to have particularly good binding properties. Others call for all-purpose flour or instant-dissolving flour, because they make a smoother stew without adding a new flavor.

You'll need some basic kitchen equipment to cook chili: a sharp knife, a cutting board, a big spoon, and a large pot (although some recipes in this book may require an extra pot or two). Some measuring equipment may come in handy.

Of course a food processor is a very convenient chili-making tool, especially if you're preparing an elaborate recipe. Another gadget, new on the market, is also quite helpful in chili preparation. Called Minichop, it is a small, hand-held food processor that does a superb job of mincing garlic, small amounts of onion, cilantro, and peppers.

Traditionally, the symbol of cooking chili has been the cast-iron Dutch oven or pot. It is still my favorite vessel for *cooking chili, but just about any pot big enough to hold the ingredients will do.*

*Cook-off competitors have pioneered the use of pots with nonstick coatings so they won't have to use additional fat. But you may choose to use one in your kitchen just to make your clean-up easier. Other cooks swear by a stainless-steel pot because it does not absorb flavors from previous batches.*

# INGREDIENTS

## CHILI POWDER, CHILI MIXES, AND BRICK CHILI

*Many brands of chili powder are on the market today, but the one that is specified by name most often by experienced chili cooks is Gebhardt's. It is a combination of ground chile peppers, oregano, cumin, and garlic. Some chili powders are redder than others; the darker powders generally use the darker, milder peppers. The powders also vary because of the proportion of spices each one contains. It's best to just experiment with various brands until you find your personal favorite.*

*A few chili recipes in this book call for pure ground chiles, and these can be hard to find, especially outside the Southwest. While there is a difference between the pure ground chiles and the chili powder, substituting the powder should not be considered a recipe for failure. Chili-making is an art, not a science, and variation and adaptation are an integral part of preparation. But do keep in mind that chili powder contains spices besides chile peppers that make its taste different from the unadorned flavor of pure ground chiles.*

*For those times when you just don't want to go to the trouble to make chili yourself, there are numerous mixes on the market. Most are seasoning blends, and usually include a thickening agent; you provide the meat and liquid. Some mixes are uninspired blends in single packets, similar to those for spaghetti and gravy mix. Others feature several different envelopes of flavorings to be mixed and mingled along with the meat. One of the first and best known is Wick Fowler's 2-Alarm Chili Mix. It is so good that, as legend has it, one competitive cook paid chemists to unlock the secret of the spice blend. Of course there are other mixes, some with only regional distribution. Again, the key is finding which one suits you best. Only experimentation with a pot of chili from a mix will satisfy your curiosity and perhaps your tastebuds.*

*Yet another form of chili comes in brick form. Found in freezer or refrigerated shelves of supermarkets, it is simply extra-thick chili that has been packaged into a brick shape. To prepare it, you just add water or other liquid when heating.*

*You also can make your own brick chili by greatly reducing the amount of liquid in the original recipe. Once the stew is cooked down, pour it into foil-wrapped loaf pans and put in the freezer, where it can be stored for up to six months. Reconstitute by adding just enough liquid to attain the desired consistency and heating thoroughly.*

## CHILE PEPPERS

*The genus* Capsicum *includes peppers ranging from the large mild, sweet bell peppers to the tiny, fiery chile pequins.*

24

Opposite: Bo Pilgrim's Chicken Chili with cornbread (p. 44)

*Because the difference in size and taste can be eye-watering, it is hard to believe that they are all cousins.*

*In general, the larger a pepper's size, the milder its bite. Smaller, narrower peppers that taper to sharp points usually are the hottest. On the Scoville scale—which has been devised to rate pepper hotness—small peppers such as Tabasco and chiles pequins rate near the top. Just below are the jalapeños, and on down the scale are ancho chiles. Still milder are paprika and pimiento.*

*The type of chile has a lot to do with the degree of hotness, but so does the climate in which it is grown. Perhaps not so coincidentally, the hotter chile peppers are the ones that mature in the hot, dry months.*

*Just about any chile can be eaten fresh or dried. Note, however, that fresh green peppers turn red as they mature and the more mature a pepper is, the hotter it is. Some peppers turn darker shades of red or even black when dried.*

*Following are descriptions of some common chiles used in chili:*

## Ancho:
*The poblano pepper in its dried state. This is the chile most often used in commercial chili powders. It is round to oblong in shape, usually 3 to 4 inches long. Its skin is wrinkled and the color ranges from deep red to blackish.*

### Arbol:

*Very hot, dried red pepper which resembles japone, but it is longer and thinner.*

### California Chile Pods:

*Long red pod, when dried. This is the dried version of the mild California Anaheim chile. Six to 8 inches long and about 1½ inches wide, it is brighter red than the ancho and is sometimes labeled "molido" in its pure ground state. It is lighter red than ancho powder.*

### Cayenne:

*Long, very slender pod, 6 to 8 inches long. Most often ground. Also known as ground red pepper. Very hot.*

### Chile Pequin:

*Very small, pea-sized, dried red chile, either round or oval in shape. Very hot.*

### Green chiles:

*Includes several varieties known as Anaheim, California, New Mexico. Longer, wider green pods, usually 4 to 8 inches long. Mild to medium hot.*

### Japone:

*Very hot dried serrano chile. This is long and slender, about 2 inches in length.*

### New Mexico Red Chile:

*Very similar in appearance to California Chile pods. These dried chiles are often hung in wreaths or chains. Usually hot.*

## Serrano:

*Slender, sharply pointed, thin-skinned chile, from 1 to 4 inches long. When dried, it is known as japone. Very hot.*

Because peppers contain capsaicin, a fiery alkaloid, in the cross walls and the inner lining, they require special handling, especially if they're fresh. The chemical that gives peppers their heat can be quite irritating to skin, eyes, and mucous membranes. Although it would require delicate surgery, you could cut out the inner lining of even a fresh jalapeño and it would be as sweet as a bell pepper, according to experts. Only after a pepper has been processed—either by drying or pickling—does the capsaicin infiltrate the outer walls and seeds of the pepper, making it hot throughout.

For safe handling, wear rubber or plastic gloves, or hold peppers with a paper towel or plastic wrap. Afterward, wash hands thoroughly and keep them away from eyes and other sensitive tissues for a couple hours.

Protecting yourself when you eat is another matter. If you take a bite of really hot chili and it proves just too scorching, reach for cheese, yogurt, sour cream, milk, or even a bit of butter. Dairy products somewhat neutralize capsaicin. A big gulp of cold water, beer, iced tea, or other water-based drinks merely moves the source of heat. Because capsaicin is insoluble in water, liquids actually force the intolerable capsaicin into your stomach. Your mouth may quit burning, but your stomach will be next.

# THINGS TO EAT WITH CHILI

**P**urists will tell you that the only thing you eat with chili is a spoon.

But let's not be picky. There are a number of traditional and non-traditional accompaniments to chili. Ironically, some are actually designed to heat things up. Others cool the chili and stretch it a bit further, or they simply provide flavor and texture contrast.

## SOME LIKE IT HOTTER

*If you want to put a little more heat in your chili, consider these accompaniments:*

- *Mexican hot sauce*
- *Chopped green, white, or yellow onions (yellow onions are the strongest)*
- *Whole, sliced, or puréed jalapeños. Serve the latter as you would a Mexican hot sauce*
- *Red pepper sauce*
- *Sliced fresh chile peppers*

## COOLING DOWN

*If your mouth could use a break, consider one of these accompaniments:*

- *Ketchup*
- *Grated cheese (Cheddar is the most traditional type, and Monterey Jack is another good choice, but any kind will do)*
- *Buttered tortilla chips or crackers (The butter also helps neutralize the heat of the chile peppers)*
- *Sugar (Add some to the chili while cooking; the sugar helps tame the heat, but be careful not to add so much that you can taste the sweetness)*

## OTHER SIDE ORDERS

*Spoon chili over rice, hash brown potatoes, mashed potatoes, spaghetti, macaroni, spaghetti squash, pinto beans, kidney beans, scrambled eggs, grits.*

*Eat alongside chili: cornbread, tortilla chips, crackers, soft flour tortillas, soft corn tortillas, biscuits, hard rolls, French bread.*

*Other garnishes: chopped or mashed avocadoes, sliced black or green olives, garbanzo beans, shredded radish, croutons, bacon bits, oyster crackers.*

# THE RIGHT STUFF

# TEXAS CHUCKWAGON CHILI

## SERVES 6 TO 8

### INGREDIENTS

3 pounds (1⅓ k) lean chuck roast,
cut into ¼-inch (¾-cm) cubes
6 tablespoons (50 g) chili powder
3 tablespoons ground oregano
6 cloves garlic, minced
3 tablespoons ground cumin
1 tablespoon cayenne pepper,
or to taste
1 to 1½ quarts (950 to 1400 mL)
water
1 to 2 teaspoons salt or to taste
⅓ cup (50 g) masa trigo, masa harina,
or cornmeal
⅓ cup (75 mL) water

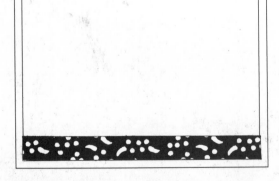

This recipe is based on an old chuckwagon recipe, used on one of Texas' largest ranches. Chuckwagons accompanied the cowboys on trail drives. This isn't a cook-off style recipe; it's purist chili con carne. Basically meat and spices, it is chili reduced to its barest essence, but it's still darn good chili.

Trim fat from edges of roast. Render enough fat from trimming to cover bottom of cast-iron Dutch oven. Remove pieces of fat. Sear the meat in the hot fat. Cook until meat loses color and most of the water given up by the meat during cooking has boiled away.

Add chili powder, oregano, garlic, cumin, and cayenne. Stir to coat meat. Add water to a level even with the meat;

Opposite: Texas Chuckwagon Chili

*stir well. Bring liquid to a boil, reduce heat, and simmer, covered, 1 to 1½ hours, or until meat is tender. Stir occasionally and add more water if necessary.*

*Add salt to taste. Make a thick paste by stirring water into masa or cornmeal. Stir to remove lumps. Gradually add to chili, stirring to prevent lumping. Simmer chili, uncovered, 30 to 45 minutes longer to thicken and reduce stew to desired consistency. Adjust seasoning as desired.*

# HOMESTYLE CHILI

## SERVES 8

### INGREDIENTS

Fat trimmed from chuck roast, coarsely chopped

3 pounds (1⅓ k) beef chuck roast, coarsely ground or cut in ¼-inch (¾-cm) cubes

6 cloves garlic, minced

6 tablespoons (50 g) chili powder

3 tablespoons ground cumin

1 to 2 teaspoons salt or to taste

2 cans (10 ounces/285 g each) enchilada sauce, mild or hot, plus 1 can water

¼ cup (35 g) masa trigo and water or ¼ cup (35 g) instant dissolving flour

*This is an uncomplicated chili recipe which gives a nice thick consistency and a flavor that's a bit more sophisticated than the simplest recipes made only with chili powder, broth or water, and meat.*

*Place approximately ¼ cup (60 g) chopped fat from roast in bottom of Dutch oven, preferably cast iron. Render enough fat to cover bottom of pot. Remove browned pieces with slotted spoons. (If using preground "chili meat," do not add additional fat. There is enough in the meat. Simply place meat in pot and proceed.)*

*Add meat and cook until meat loses color. Cook long enough to evaporate the water released by the beef, but do not brown.*

Add garlic and stir to release aroma. Add chili powder, cumin, and salt to taste. Stir to coat meat with spices.

Add enchilada sauce and water or beef broth. Bring to a boil. Reduce heat, cover, and simmer for 1 hour or until meat is tender. Adjust seasoning.

Add just enough water (approximately ¼ cup/ 60 mL) to masa to make a smooth paste. Press out all lumps with back of a spoon. Gradually, add masa paste or instant flour to chili, stirring constantly. Cook, uncovered, until thickened and flavors mellow, 10 to 15 minutes more.

## Note

*If enchilada sauce is not available, use 2 cans (14½ ounces/400 g each) beef broth. A bit more thickening may be needed. If a hotter chili is desired, add cayenne pepper to taste.*

# FAVORITE CHILI

## SERVES 10 TO 12

INGREDIENTS

4 dried chiles anchos
4 dried chiles arbols
2 dried chiles japones
3 teaspoons cumin seed
7 cloves garlic
1 teaspoon crushed chiles pequins
5 fresh jalapeño peppers,
stemmed and seeded
1 pound (450 g) tomatoes, canned
or fresh, undrained
2 teaspoons salt
Fat trimmed from beef or ¼ pound
(115 g) chopped beef suet
4 pounds (1¾ k) lean beef, such as
trimmed chuck roast or chuck tender,
cut in ¼-inch (¾-cm) cubes
1 teaspoon sugar
1 cup (240 mL) red wine
2 to 3 cups (425 to 700 mL) water,
approximately
¼ cup (35 g) masa trigo

*This chili is a project; it takes nearly all day by the time you've shopped for and found the fresh and dried chiles, softened them, and proceeded with the rest of the recipe. But it's worth it. If you can't find these exact chiles, don't be afraid to experiment with what's available or your own combinations. Mexican markets usually have a wide variety of dried and fresh chiles.*

*Remove stems, membranes, and seeds from dried chiles (anchos, arbols, japones). Place in small saucepan and barely cover with water. Bring to a boil over medium heat and simmer 15 minutes. Remove peppers from liquid and set aside. Reserve liquid and add to chili sparingly as desired for a hotter stew.*

*Place softened peppers in food processor along with cumin, garlic, chiles pequins, jalapeños, tomatoes, and salt. Process until smooth.*

*Meanwhile, in a cast-iron pot or Dutch oven, render enough fat from trimmings or suet to make ¼ cup (60 mL). Cook meat in rendered fat over high heat until meat loses color and turns gray. Cook meat in 2 batches if pot is crowded. Cook away most of the water the meat gives up, but do not brown.*

*To meat, add pepper and tomato mixture, sugar, and wine. Add just enough water to raise level of liquid to that of meat. Do not cover completely with liquid. Bring to a boil, reduce heat, and simmer uncovered, about 1½ hours, stirring occasionally. Add water as needed to maintain desired level.*

*Combine masa trigo and just enough water to make a smooth paste. Press out all lumps with the back of a spoon. Gradually stir into chili to thicken. Taste for seasoning and adjust. If a hotter chili is desired, add a bit of reserved chili liquid. Cook about 30 minutes longer over very low heat, stirring frequently.*

# DEEP HOLE CHILI

## SERVES 10 TO 12

### DRILLING MUD
2 chiles anchos, stemmed
3 chiles japones
1 tablespoon cumin seed, ground by hand
4½ teaspoons ground oregano
1 tablespoon red wine vinegar
3 large cloves garlic, chopped fine
1 tablespoon paprika
2 tablespoons chopped fresh cilantro
1 teaspoon sugar
1 teaspoon black pepper
2 teaspoons salt
4 cups (950 mL) water

♥

### CRUDE INGREDIENTS
2 pounds (900 g) large, sweet onions,
quartered and sliced
2 tablespoons vegetable oil
¾ pound (340 g) beef suet, ground
4 pounds (1¾ k) venison or beef chuck
tender, cut in ¼- to ½-inch (¾- to 1½-cm)
cubes
1 can (10¾ ounces/300 g) beef broth
2 pounds (900 g) canned, whole tomatoes,
coarsely chopped
2 bay leaves
Up to 5 tablespoons (50 g) chili powder or to
taste
1 tablespoon mole sauce (optional)
2 tablespoons (15 g) masa harina dissolved in
2 tablespoons water, if needed

*This is the recipe used by competitive chili cooks Rock Grundman and Scott Nickson who are in the Texas "ahl bidniz." They work for Dresser Industries, one of the world's largest oilfield equipment suppliers. They call it Deep Hole Chili. When they're cooking for prizes, they use beef. When they're cooking for pleasure, they use venison.*

*Add first 11 ingredients to 4 cups (950 mL) water in a large saucepan. Bring to a boil, reduce heat and simmer, uncovered, 30 minutes. Purée Drilling Mud mixture in food processor or blender.*

*Meanwhile, in large skillet, sauté onions in oil until transparent. Transfer onions to large Dutch oven or chili* pot. Combine ground suet and cubed venison or beef and cook in small batches in skillet until meat loses color. Transfer meat to chili pot.

Pour beef broth into skillet and heat to boiling. Scrape bottom of skillet to loosen browned particles and pour broth into chili pot. Add tomatoes and bay leaves to chili pot. Bring to a boil, reduce heat, and simmer, covered, 1 hour.

Add Drilling Mud mixture, chili powder, and mole sauce. Simmer, uncovered, 1 to 4 hours, until meat is tender and stew is thickened. If desired, thicken with a smooth paste of masa and water, 2 tablespoons (15 g) of each, toward end of cooking time.

Adjust seasoning after first hour of cooking. Longer cooking time depends on when you want to eat and what time you have to turn in the meat for judging.

This chili gets better after a night in the refrigerator. Skim any excess fat.

# VENISON CHILI

## SERVES 8

### INGREDIENTS

1 pound (450 g) coarsely ground beef for chili (chili grind)

2 pounds (900 g) coarsely ground venison (chili grind)

1 large onion, chopped

4 cloves garlic, minced

¼ cup (35 g) chili powder

1 tablespoon ground cumin

1 can (8 ounces/225 g) tomato sauce

1 can (6 ounces/175 g) tomato paste

2 cups (425 mL) water

2 teaspoons brown sugar

2 teaspoons salt

1 can (15 ounces/425 g) pinto beans or pinto beans with jalapeño peppers (optional)

2 tablespoons instant flour or
2 tablespoons masa trigo mixed with water to make a smooth paste (optional)

Cayenne pepper to taste

*Venison makes very good chili because the lean meat stays firm during prolonged cooking. Mixed with beef, the flavor is rich and meaty.*

*Place beef in cast-iron pot or Dutch oven and cook over high heat until meat starts to release fat and juices. Add venison and cook until meat loses color and most of the liquid cooks away. Do not brown. Drain excess fat if necessary.*

*Add onion and cook until onion is soft. Stir in garlic and cook briefly to release aroma. Add chili powder and cumin; stir to coat meat. Add tomato sauce, tomato paste, water, brown sugar, and salt. Reduce heat, cover, and simmer 1½ hours. Add beans, if desired. (Purists will want to serve beans on the side.)*

*If chili needs thickening, stir in instant flour or masa paste and adjust seasoning. Add cayenne pepper to taste if a spicier chili is desired. Stir and cook 30 minutes longer.*

Opposite: New Mexico Green Chile Stew (p. 45)

Nancy Parker, of Greenville, Texas, is an expert in the use of a food processor and is one of the most popular cooking teachers in the Southwest. Her specialty is elegant, but easy entertaining and this dressed up version of chili is typical of the style that has earned her a devoted following.

Using steel blade of food processor, chop beef cubes 1 cup (225 g) at a time in food processor (using pulse motion) to get a coarse grind of meat for chili. In large pot, sauté onions in suet or oil until golden brown, remove, and set aside. Add beef and cook until gray.

Return onions to pot and stir in tomatoes, garlic, Burgundy, chili powder, oregano, basil, and cumin. Bring liquid to boil, reduce heat, cover and simmer for 45 minutes.

Add olives and pecans and simmer, uncovered, for 10 minutes longer. Add beans, if desired. Add salt to taste. If possible, make a day ahead and refrigerate overnight. Skim off any excess fat. Garnish with chopped parsley or cilantro.

# NANCY PARKER'S TEXAS GOURMET CHILI

**SERVES 8 TO 10**

INGREDIENTS

3 pounds (1⅓ k) beef chuck, cut in 1-inch (2½-cm) cubes
6 medium onions, thinly sliced
¾ cup (175 g) chopped beef suet or ⅓ cup (75 mL) vegetable oil
3 cans (14½ ounces/400 g each) sliced baby tomatoes, undrained
3 cloves garlic, minced
¾ cup (175 mL) Burgundy wine
⅓ cup (50 g) chili powder
½ teaspoon ground oregano
½ teaspoon leaf basil
1 teaspoon ground cumin
⅓ cup (40 g) chopped pitted ripe olives
½ cup (60 g) chopped pecans
1 cup (115 g) drained kidney beans (optional)
Salt to taste
Chopped fresh cilantro or parsley

# ON THE BORDER

## BO PILGRIM'S CHICKEN CHILI

### SERVES 4 TO 6

INGREDIENTS

1 medium onion, chopped
2 cloves garlic, chopped
¼ cup (60 mL) vegetable oil
1 (2-pound/900-g) whole boneless
chicken or 2 pounds (900 g)
boneless, skinned chicken breasts,
coarsely chopped
¼ cup (35 g) chili powder
2 tablespoons ground cumin
½ teaspoon cayenne pepper
1 teaspoon salt
2 tablespoons flour
1 can (8 ounces/225 g) tomato sauce
1½ cups (350 mL) water
1 teaspoon sugar

*Bo Pilgrim raises chickens—a lot of them—in the East Texas town of Pittsburg. He invented a device that will bone a whole chicken, and this is his prize-winning chili recipe in which he uses his boneless chicken.*

*Cook onion and garlic in oil in large pot over medium-high heat 5 minutes or until soft. Add chicken and cook until chicken is no longer transparent. Add chili powder, cumin, cayenne, and salt. Stir to coat meat. Add flour; stir again.*

*Pour in tomato sauce and water; add sugar. Reduce heat, cover, and simmer 30 minutes. Remove lid and simmer another 20 to 30 minutes, until chili is thickened and meat is tender.*

New Mexicans like to use green chiles to make what is a good, robust stew. Every New Mexican has a version and there are "green chile" cook-offs in New Mexico, just as there are chili cook-offs in Texas and other states all over the union. Don't look for chili powder; you won't find any. Serve it with or without beans on the side.

Trim fat from pork. Cut pork or beef into ¼-inch (¾-cm) cubes. Brown in vegetable oil in medium pot. Add onion and cook 5 minutes or until soft. Add garlic, tomatoes and green chiles, chopped green chiles, cumin, and water. Use just enough water to raise liquid to level of meat.

Season to taste with salt and pepper. Bring liquid to a boil, reduce heat, cover, and simmer 1 hour, until meat is tender. Remove lid and simmer until stew is thick and rich looking, 15 to 20 minutes longer. Stir frequently.

# NEW MEXICO GREEN CHILE STEW

## SERVES 4

### INGREDIENTS

1 pound (450 g) boneless pork butt, beef chuck tender, or rump roast
1 tablespoon vegetable oil
1 medium onion, chopped
2 cloves garlic, minced
1 can (10½ ounces/300 g) tomatoes and green chiles, undrained and coarsely chopped
1 can (4 ounces/115 g) seeded and chopped green chiles
¼ teaspoon ground cumin
1 cup (240 mL) water
Salt and pepper to taste

# CHOCOLATE CHILI

## SERVES 4

### INGREDIENTS

2 pounds (900 g) beef chuck tender or beef round, coarsely cubed

1 pound (450 g) pork loin, coarsely cubed

Fat trimmings from beef and pork, rendered to make ¼ cup (60 mL) fat (add oil if necessary)

1 onion, chopped

2 cloves garlic, minced

1 tablespoon flour

3 tablespoons chili powder

1¼ teaspoons salt

1 tablespoon ground cumin

1 can (29 ounces/825 g) puréed tomatoes

¼ teaspoon ground cinnamon

4½ teaspoons sugar

1 square (1 ounce/30 g) unsweetened baking chocolate

*Many chili cooks swear that adding a touch of chocolate is the secret to making good chili. This is not a nouvelle contrivance. Mexican cuisine has been combining red chiles with chocolate in mole sauce for centuries.*

*In Dutch oven, cook beef and pork in rendered fat over medium-high heat until meat begins to lose color. Cook away most of liquid which forms in bottom of pot. Add onion and garlic; cook 5 minutes or until onions are soft.*

*Sprinkle flour, chili powder, salt, and cumin over meat. Stir to coat meat well. Add tomatoes. Cover and simmer 1 to 1½ hours. Remove from heat and allow to cool to serving temperature. Add cinnamon, sugar, and chocolate. Stir to melt chocolate and dissolve sugar. Serve immediately. If needed, reheat gently. Do not cook over high heat to avoid burning chocolate.*

Cook pork in oil in medium pot until pork begins to brown. Add onion and garlic and cook 5 minutes or until onion is transparent. Stir in flour, chili powder, cumin, salt, and pepper. Stir to coat meat.

Stir in tomatoes and tomato sauce. Simmer, uncovered, 1 hour or until pork is tender and stew is thickened.

# PORK CHILI

### SERVES 4 TO 6

INGREDIENTS

1½ pounds (600 g) boneless pork, cut into 1-inch (2½-cm) cubes

1 tablespoon vegetable oil

1 medium onion, coarsely chopped

1 clove garlic, crushed

1 tablespoon all-purpose flour

¼ cup (35 g) chili powder

1 tablespoon ground cumin

1 teaspoon salt

½ teaspoon pepper

2 cans (16 ounces/450 g each) whole peeled tomatoes, cut up

1 can (8 ounces/225 g) tomato sauce

# ALL-BEAN CHILI

## SERVES 12

INGREDIENTS

2 cups (340 g) dry pinto beans
5 to 6 cups (1200 to 1400 mL) water
2 tablespoons vegetable oil
1 onion, chopped
2 cloves garlic, minced
1 fresh jalapeño pepper, seeded and chopped
2 tablespoons chili powder
2 teaspoons ground cumin
1 cup (115 g) chopped fresh tomato
1 can (15½ to 16 ounces/450 g) yellow hominy, drained
2 teaspoons salt
¼ cup (7 g) chopped fresh cilantro
1 teaspoon sugar

*In Texas, much ado is made about whether chili should have beans. Most everybody agrees it shouldn't, at least when the chili is made of meat. But this version eliminates that controversy. It's all beans, no meat.*

*Rinse beans, place in saucepan, and cover with 2 cups (425 mL) water. Remove any blemished or shriveled beans that float to the top. Soak beans overnight or bring water to a boil, turn off heat, cover, and let beans sit 1 hour.*

*Add enough water to cover beans ½ inch (1½ cm)—3 to 4 cups (700 to 950 mL), depending on whether they've been soaked or pre-cooked. Add oil, chopped onion, garlic, jalapeño, chili powder, and cumin.*

*Bring water to a boil. Reduce heat, cover, and simmer 1½ to 2 hours, until beans are tender. Add tomato, hominy, salt, cilantro, and sugar. Cook 30 minutes more, uncovered, until mixture thickens. Serve as side dish or vegetarian main course.*

Opposite: All-Bean Chili

This is a mild hamburger-style chili, common in America's heartland. It's closer to Texas chili than that made in Cincinnati. The first time my husband, a Kansas City native, ate my Texas chili, he called it a "cruel joke." Since then, he's come to prefer the hotter, Lone Star versions.

Cook meat in large, heavy pot or Dutch oven over high heat, until meat loses color. Add onion and cook 5 minutes or until onion is soft. Add garlic; stir to release aroma.

Add chili powder, cumin, and salt. Stir to coat meat. Add tomatoes, breaking into pieces with back of slotted spoon. Add tomato sauce, 1/2 cup water (125 mL), or enough to barely cover meat, and sugar. Cover and simmer 30 minutes. Taste and adjust seasoning, adding red pepper sauce, if desired. Remove lid and simmer another 30 to 45 minutes, adding a small amount of water, if necessary to prevent sticking. Cook until meat is tender. Add beans about 15 minutes before end of cooking time.

# KANSAS CITY CHILI

## SERVES 8 TO 10

### INGREDIENTS

2 pounds (900 g) ground beef
1 large onion, chopped
2 cloves garlic, minced
1/4 cup (35 g) chili powder
1 tablespoon ground cumin
2 teaspoons salt
1 can (28 ounces/800 g) peeled whole tomatoes
1 can (8 ounces/225 g) tomato sauce
1/2 cup (125 mL) water, approximately
1 teaspoon sugar
Red pepper sauce, if desired
1 can (16 ounces/450 g) red kidney beans, drained

# CINCINNATI CHILI

## SERVES 6 TO 8

### INGREDIENTS

2 cups (425 mL) beef broth
2 pounds (900 g) ground beef
1 onion, chopped
¼ cup (35 g) chili powder
½ teaspoon ground cinnamon
1 teaspoon ground cumin
1 teaspoon garlic powder
½ teaspoon salt
½ teaspoon turmeric
½ teaspoon ground coriander
¼ teaspoon ground allspice
pinch of cayenne pepper
1 tablespoon paprika
1 teaspoon sugar
1 bay leaf
1 can (15 ounces/425 g) tomato sauce
2 tablespoons cider vinegar
12 to 16 ounces (340-450 g)
spaghetti, cooked and drained
Oyster crackers
Shredded cheese
Chopped onion
Kidney beans, heated

*Spaghetti, oyster crackers, and ground beef are the distinguishing characteristics of the style of chili known as Cincinnati Chili. Also known as Empress Chili for the local chain that made it famous, Cincinnati chili comes several different "ways." It is always served over spaghetti with shredded cheese on top and oyster crackers on the side. That's "three-way chili." Add chopped onion and you've got "four-way chili." Throw in some kidney beans and you're enjoying "five-way chili."*

*Place beef broth in a Dutch oven or stewpot and bring to a boil. Slowly add beef to broth until meat separates into very small pieces. Break up any chunks. Reduce heat, cover, and simmer 30 minutes.*

*Add onion, chili powder, cinnamon, cumin, garlic powder, salt, turmeric, coriander, allspice, cayenne, paprika, sugar, bay leaf, tomato sauce, and vinegar. Bring to a boil. Reduce heat and simmer, covered, 30 minutes, stirring occasionally. Remove lid and simmer another 30 minutes, stirring frequently. Chili should be the consistency of a meat sauce for spaghetti.*

*If time allows, refrigerate overnight. Skim off fat before reheating. Serve over cooked spaghetti, with cheese, oyster crackers, cheese, onion, and kidney beans, if desired.*

# BIG MAMA'S OKLAHOMA CHILI

## SERVES 8 TO 10

INGREDIENTS

3 tablespoons safflower oil
1 large onion, chopped
3 cloves garlic, minced
4 to 5 pounds (2 kg) lean chuck,
coarsely ground
¼ cup (35 g) chili powder mixed
with ½ cup (125 mL) water
3 or 4 dried chiles pequins, ground
by hand in a mortar and pestle
¼ teaspoon ground cumin
1 tablespoon ground oregano
3 cans (6 ounces/175 g) tomato paste
3 to 4 cans (15 ounces/425 g)
plain pinto beans
Salt and pepper to taste
Water

*Amber Robinson has a cooking school in Dallas and offers sophisticated classes for sophisticated cooks. But she hasn't forgotten her native state, Oklahoma, and its traditional food. She calls this "North of the Red River Chili" and says it's a particular favorite with little children and pinto bean lovers.*

*In a 6-quart (6-L), heavy pan, heat oil and sauté onion and garlic until soft. Add ground beef and cook until meat loses color. Add chili powder mixture, ground chiles pequins, cumin, oregano, and tomato paste. Simmer about 15 minutes, until seasonings and tomato paste are well blended.*

*Add beans, salt, and pepper and cover with just enough water to barely cover meat and beans. Cover and simmer about 2 hours.*

# CHAMPIONSHIP SEASONINGS

# FRANK TOLBERT'S ORIGINAL TEXAS CHILI

## SERVES 4 TO 6

### INGREDIENTS

2 to 4 chiles anchos or 4 to 8 chiles japones (see note)

3 pounds (1⅓ kg) lean beef chuck, such as chuck tender, cut into bite-sized pieces

2 ounces (60 g) beef kidney suet, finely chopped, or 4 tablespoons vegetable oil (60 mL), divided

Water or beef broth, approximately 1 to 2 cups (240-425 mL)

⅓ cup (40 g) finely chopped garlic

1 onion, finely chopped (optional)

2 tablespoons ground cumin

1 tablespoon ground oregano

Salt to taste

½ cup (70 g) paprika

1 to 2 stems fresh cilantro, chopped (optional)

*The late Frank Tolbert was the godfather, guru, spiritual leader and chief rabble rouser of the modern chili movement. Tolbert, a columnist for* The Dallas Morning News *until his death in January, 1984, was one of the founders of the championship chili cook-off in Terlingua. This recipe was given for use by his daughter, Kathleen Tolbert Ryan. His writings did much to popularize chili far beyond the borders of his native state.*

*Trim stems from anchos or japones. Remove seeds from anchos. Place in small saucepan and barely cover with water. Bring water to a boil, remove from heat, cover, and soak chiles for 15 minutes. Place soaking water and peppers in blender or*

food processor and purée until smooth.

Cook half the beef with half the suet or 2 tablespoons vegetable oil in a large skillet over high heat until meat loses color and appears gray.

When meat is gray, pour accumulated liquid from skillet into a large Dutch oven or stew pot along with the puréed pepper mixture. Place over low heat and simmer. Meanwhile, add remaining suet or oil and rest of beef to the skillet and cook until meat is brown and almost dry.

Add rest of meat to chili pot and add water or beef broth to level of meat. Bring liquid to a boil, reduce heat, and simmer, uncovered, for 30 minutes. Add garlic, onion, cumin, oregano, salt, paprika, and cilantro; simmer for another 30 minutes or until meat is very tender. Add a bit more liquid if chili starts to stick or too much liquid cooks away. Stir occasionally.

Remove from heat and let chili rest overnight, refrigerated. Skim off excess fat, if any, in the morning. Reheat and serve.

## Note

If dried chiles are not available, substitute 1 heaping tablespoon chili powder per pod.

# CHAMPIONSHIP CHILI

## SERVES 32

### INGREDIENTS

4 pounds (1¾ kg) flank steak
5 pounds (2¼ kg) thin, center-cut pork chops
6 green chiles, roasted, peeled, and seeded;
or 6 canned whole green chiles, seeded
2 teaspoons sugar
3 teaspoons ground oregano
3 teaspoons ground cumin
½ teaspoon monosodium glutamate (MSG)
(optional)
3 teaspoons black pepper
4 teaspoons salt
5 tablespoons (50 g) chili powder
1 teaspoon chopped fresh cilantro
1 teaspoon ground thyme
1 cup (240 mL) beer
4 cans (15 to 16 ounces/425 g each)
whole tomatoes, coarsely chopped
¼ cup (30 g) finely chopped celery
2 cloves garlic, finely chopped
3 medium onions, cut into ½-inch
(1½-cm) pieces
2 green peppers, cut into ⅜-inch
(1¼-cm) pieces
1½ quarts (1¼-L) chicken broth
½ pound (225 g) beef kidney suet, chopped,
or ½ cup (125 mL) cooking oil, divided
1 pound (450 g) Monterey Jack cheese,
shredded
1 lime

*Before the first great schism in the chili world, C. V. Wood Jr., a Californian, won 2 championships at Terlingua. After the split, Wood led his followers to California with the International Chili Society where the "world championship" is held annually. This recipe is an adaptation of C. V. Wood Jr.'s 1969 and 1971 Championship Chili.*

*Trim any fat from flank steak and cut it into ⅜-inch (1¼-cm) cubes. Trim all fat and bones from pork and cut it into ¼-inch (¾-cm) cubes. Combine meats and set aside.*

*Cut green chiles into ¼-inch (¾-cm) squares; reserve. Mix sugar, oregano, cumin, MSG, pepper, salt, chili powder, cilantro, and thyme with beer in large bowl until all lumps are dissolved. Add the tomatoes, celery, garlic, onions, green peppers, green chiles, and beer mixture to the chicken broth in large stewpot or Dutch oven and begin heating.*

*Place ⅓ of the suet or oil, along with ⅓ of the pork and beef mixture, in a skillet and sear meat. Cook until meat loses color. Add to broth mixture. Repeat with remaining meat and suet or oil until all meat is seared. Combine with broth mixture.*

*Bring chili to a boil, reduce heat, cover, and simmer 1 hour. Remove lid and cook 2 hours longer until meat is tender, about to break down. If time allows, cool chili and refrigerate 24 hours to allow the seasonings to meld. Reheat to serve.*

*About 5 minutes before serving, add shredded cheese to chili, stirring to dissolve completely. (To serve in batches, use ⅛ pound/60 g of cheese to each quart.)*

*Immediately before serving, add the juice of one lime.*

# CARROLL SHELBY'S CELEBRITY CHILI

## SERVES 4 TO 6

### INGREDIENTS

1 pound (450 g) round steak or coarsely ground beef for chili
1 pound (450 g) beef chuck steak
½ cup (125 mL) vegetable oil
1 can (8 ounces/225 g) tomato sauce
1 can (12 ounces/340 g) beer
¼ cup (35 g) chili powder
1½ teaspoons minced garlic
1 teaspoon chopped onion
1¼ teaspoons oregano leaves
Scant ½ teaspoon paprika
1¼ teaspoons salt
1 teaspoon ground cumin
1 teaspoon cayenne pepper, or to taste
½ to ¾ pound goat cheese, grated
½ teaspoon cumin seed

*Carroll Shelby is undoubtedly better known as a race car driver and the developer of the Ford Mustang Cobra. But he is also one of the originators of the Terlingua championship chili cook-off and a member of the board of governors of the International Chili Society. Shelby also has his own chili mix company. Here is a version he calls his celebrity chili.*

*In skillet, sear beef in oil until brown. Transfer meat to a 2-quart (2-L) cast iron pot. Add tomato sauce and beer; bring liquid to a boil. Meanwhile, add chili powder, garlic, onion, oregano, paprika, salt, and cumin. Cover, reduce heat, and simmer 1 hour, stirring occasionally.*

*Add cayenne and simmer, covered, 2 hours longer, stirring often. Add goat cheese and cumin seed and stir frequently while cooking, uncovered, another 30 minutes.*

This is Fred Drexel's 1981 *International Chili Society World Championship Chili.*

*In a large cast-iron kettle or Dutch oven, brown beef, pork, and onion in oil. Add salt and pepper to taste. Add remaining ingredients and stir well. Cover and simmer 3 to 4 hours, until meat is tender and chili is thick and bubbly. Remove lid during last hour of cooking to thicken, if needed. Stir occasionally.*

# 1981 CHILI SOCIETY WINNER

## SERVES 4 TO 6

INGREDIENTS

2½ pounds (1 kg) beef brisket,
cut in 1-inch cubes
1 pound (450 g) lean ground pork
1 large onion, finely chopped
2 tablespoons vegetable oil
Salt and pepper to taste
2 to 3 cloves garlic, minced
2 tablespoons seeded and diced
green chiles
1 can (8 ounces/225 g) tomato sauce
1 beef bouillon cube
1 can (12 ounces/340 g) beer
1¼ cups (300 mL) water
4 to 6 tablespoons (35-60 g)
chili powder
2½ tablespoons ground cumin
⅛ teaspoon dry mustard
⅛ teaspoon brown sugar
Pinch of ground oregano

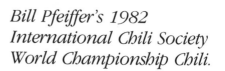

# 1982
# CHILI SOCIETY
# WINNER

## SERVES 24 TO 32

### INGREDIENTS

1 tablespoon ground oregano
2 tablespoons paprika
2 tablespoons monosodium glutamate (MSG) (optional)
11 tablespoons chili powder
¼ cup ground cumin
¼ cup (35 g) instant beef bouillon, crushed
3 cans (12 ounces/340 g each) beer
2 cups (425 mL) or more water
2 pounds (900 g) thick butterfly pork chops, cubed
2 pounds (900 g) beef chuck, cubed
6 pounds (2¾ kg) ground beef rump roast
½ cup (125 mL) vegetable oil or chopped kidney suet, divided
4 large onions, finely chopped
10 cloves garlic, finely chopped
1 teaspoon powdered mole
1 tablespoon sugar
2 teaspoons ground coriander
1 teaspoon red pepper sauce
1 can (8 ounces/225 g) tomato sauce
1 tablespoon masa harina plus 1 tablespoon warm water
Salt to taste

*Bill Pfeiffer's 1982 International Chili Society World Championship Chili.*

*In a large pot, combine oregano, paprika, MSG, chili powder, cumin, beef bouillon, beer, and 2 cups (425 mL) water. Bring to a boil, reduce heat, and simmer. In a separate skillet, sear meat in batches, using a bit of oil or chopped suet as needed, until meat is light brown. Drain meat and add to simmering spices. Continue until all meat has been cooked and added, reserving 1 tablespoon oil or suet.*

*Sauté onions and garlic in 1 tablespoon oil or kidney suet. Add to meat mixture. Add enough water to raise liquid to level of meat. Cover and simmer 2 hours. Add mole, sugar, coriander, red pepper sauce, and tomato sauce. Remove lid and simmer 45 minutes longer.*

*Dissolve masa harina in warm water to make a smooth paste and add to chili. Season with salt to taste. Simmer 30 minutes. For hotter chili, add additional red pepper sauce to taste.*

# 1983 CHILI SOCIETY WINNER

## SERVES 12 TO 14

### INGREDIENTS

2 cups (425 mL) warm water
1 tablespoon sugar
1 cup (240 mL) beef consommé
2 teaspoons ground oregano
2 tablespoons paprika
2 tablespoons ground cumin
1 tablespoon celery salt
7 tablespoons chili powder
2 tablespoons monosodium glutamate (MSG) (optional)
1 teaspoon cayenne pepper
1 teaspoon garlic powder
1 tablespoon mole paste
Vegetable oil
2 pounds (900 g) beef chuck, cut in ⅜-inch (1¼-cm) cubes
2 pounds (900 g) top round of beef, coarsely ground
2 pounds (900 g) pork butt, medium grind
3 cups (340 g) finely minced onion
2 tablespoons garlic, finely minced
1 cup (115 g) seeded and chopped green chiles
1 can (15 ounces/425 g) tomato sauce
1 can (12 ounces/340 g) beer
¼ cup (40 g) masa harina mixed with ¼ cup (60 mL) warm water, approximately

*Harold R. Timber's 1983 International Chili Society World Championship Chili.*

*Combine first 12 ingredients in large cooking pot. Stir to dissolve. Bring liquid to a boil, reduce heat, and simmer.*

*Pour just enough vegetable oil into a large skillet to lightly coat the bottom. Over high heat, sauté beef and pork, in 3 batches, using additional oil as needed. Transfer meat to larger pot and continue simmering.*

*Adding additional oil as needed, sauté onion and garlic 10 minutes or until onion is soft. Add to meat mixture along with green chiles and tomato sauce. Bring stew to a boil and pour in beer.*

*Reduce heat and simmer,
uncovered, for about 1½ to
2 hours, stirring occasionally.
If thicker chili is desired,
make a smooth paste by
combining masa harina and
warm water. Gradually add
to simmering chili until chili
is thickened to desired
consistency. Simmer 5 to
10 minutes longer. Remove
from heat and let stand for
30 minutes. Skim off excess
grease. Correct seasoning to
taste. Cover and let stand
1 hour before serving.*

# 1984
# CHILI SOCIETY
# WINNER

## SERVES 6 TO 8

INGREDIENTS

2 pounds (900 g) coarsely ground
beef for chili
1 cup (240 mL) water
1 can (16 ounces/450 g) whole
tomatoes, puréed
1 onion, finely chopped
1 teaspoon garlic powder
1 teaspoon red pepper sauce
¼ cup (35 g) chili powder
1 teaspoon ground oregano
1½ teaspoons salt
2 teaspoons ground cumin
½ teaspoon cayenne pepper
1 can (12 ounces/340 g) beer

*Dusty Hudspeth's 1984 International Chili Society World Championship Chili.*

*Cook meat over high heat in a 2-quart (2-L) heavy pan until meat loses color. Add water, puréed tomatoes, onion, and garlic powder. Bring liquid to a boil, reduce heat, cover and simmer for 30 minutes, stirring occasionally.*

*Add red pepper sauce, chili powder, oregano, salt, cumin, cayenne, and beer; stir well. Simmer, uncovered, 1 hour longer, or until meat is tender and stew is thickened.*

Opposite: Chili Cornbread (p. 76)

*This is Bill "Ice-T" Douglas' 1981
Terlingua Championship Chili.*

*Trim fat and cut meat into pieces the
size of sugar cubes. Place meat in
nonstick pan and cook over
medium-high heat until meat begins
to brown. Add ¼ teaspoon MSG.*

*Add enough water to barely cover
meat. Bring liquid to a boil, reduce
heat, and simmer vigorously,
uncovered, for 1 hour. Add tomato
sauce, cover, and simmer for 1 hour
longer. Add more water if liquid
begins to cook away.*

*Combine chili powder, cumin,
oregano, ¼ teaspoon garlic powder
and ½ teaspoon MSG, and basil (for
aroma), if desired. Meanwhile,
remove chili from heat and let cool
slightly. Stir in combined spices and
return to heat. Simmer, uncovered,
for 1 hour or longer or until meat is
tender. Add water if necessary to
prevent liquid from cooking away.*

# HURRICANE BILLY'S CHILI

### SERVES 4 TO 6

INGREDIENTS

3 pounds (1⅓ kg) arm roast
(beef shank), cubed
½ teaspoon garlic powder, divided
1 medium onion, chopped
1½ teaspoons red pepper sauce
2 teaspoons salt
1 teaspoon monosodium glutamate
(MSG), divided
Water
1 can (8 ounces/225 g) tomato sauce
4½ to 5 tablespoons (50 g)
chili powder
¾ tablespoon ground cumin
¼ teaspoon ground oregano
Pinch of ground basil (optional)

# 1982 TERLINGUA WINNER

## SERVES 6 TO 8

INGREDIENTS

3 pounds (1⅓ kg) beef chuck or
round steak, cubed
1 can (8 ounces/225 g) tomato sauce
(optional)
1 medium onion, chopped
Water
4 tablespoons chili powder
1 teaspoon garlic powder
1 teaspoon paprika
2 teaspoons salt
2 tablespoons ground cumin
¼ teaspoon cayenne pepper
½ teaspoon ground oregano
1 teaspoon monosodium glutamate
(MSG) (optional)
1 teaspoon black pepper
1 teaspoon brown sugar

*Tom Skipper's Ol' Blue Chili 1982 Terlingua Championship Chili.*

*Place meat, tomato sauce, and onion in large pot, preferably one with a non-stick surface. Add enough water to cover ingredients ½ inch (1½ cm). Bring to a boil, cover, reduce heat, and cook until meat is tender, 2 to 2½ hours, depending on tenderness of cut of meat used. Stir occasionally and add water as needed to prevent liquid from cooking away. Liquid should cook down to the level of the meat.*

*When meat is tender, stir in spices and brown sugar, cover, and cook an additional 20 to 30 minutes.*

*Paul Brian's 1983 CASI Terlingua Championship Chili.*

*Place onions in food processor along with 1 cup (240 mL) water. Process until onions are consistency of applesauce. Pierce the skins of jalapeño peppers, but do not slice. Seeds should not fall out of peppers. Place onion purée, peppers, meat, and garlic in a large pot, preferably with a non-stick surface, and cook over high heat until meat turns gray. Cover and simmer 30 minutes. Remove jalapeño peppers and discard.*

*Add tomato sauce, cover, and simmer another 30 minutes. Meanwhile, blend chili powder, cumin, salt, cayenne, ground oregano, and dry mustard. After meat has cooked a total of 1 hour, fold spice blend into pot. Add water as needed to bring liquid to level of meat. Cover and simmer 1 hour longer or until meat is tender.*

*If chili needs thickening, gradually stir in more chili powder to tighten stew to desired consistency.*

# 1983 TERLINGUA WINNER

## SERVES 10 TO 12

INGREDIENTS

1 large yellow Spanish onion, cut into large chunks

1 large red onion, cut into large chunks

1 cup (240 mL) plus additional water as needed

5 to 6 fresh jalapeño peppers

4 pounds (1¾ kg) trimmed (½ inch/ 1½ cm thick) beef round steak, coarsely ground or cut in chunks the size of a sugar cube

3 cloves garlic, minced

2 cans (8 ounces/225 g each) tomato sauce

10 tablespoons (85 g) or more chili powder

2 tablespoons ground cumin

4 teaspoons salt

1½ teaspoons cayenne pepper

1 teaspoon ground oregano

1 teaspoon dry mustard

# SILVER BULLET CHILI

## SERVES 8 TO 10

INGREDIENTS

1 medium onion, chopped
3 pounds (1⅓ kg) beef chuck, chuck tender or stew meat, cubed
Water
1 can (8 ounces/225 g) tomato sauce
¼ cup (35 g) paprika
1 teaspoon black pepper
½ teaspoon cayenne pepper
1½ teaspoons salt or to taste
¼ cup (35 g) chili powder
1 tablespoon ground cumin
1 teaspoon garlic powder

*David Talbot's 1983 Original Terlingua International Frank X. Tolbert–Wick Fowler Memorial Championship Chili.*

*Sauté onion and meat in large pot 5 minutes or until onion is soft and meat loses color. Add just enough water to barely cover meat. Bring liquid to boil, reduce heat, cover, and simmer until meat is tender, about 1 to 1½ hours, depending on tenderness of cut of meat used. Liquid should cook down somewhat.*

*Add remaining ingredients and stir well. Cook uncovered an additional 15 minutes.*

*This is Steve Weaver's 1984 CASI Terlingua Championship Chili.*

*Melt lard or drippings in large pot over medium heat. Add onion and cook until translucent. Add meat and garlic and cook until meat is quite brown.*

*Add tomato sauce, ground red chile peppers, chili powder, cumin, and salt. Stir to coat meat. Add just enough water to cover meat. Bring to a boil, reduce heat, cover, and simmer 2 to 2¼ hours, stirring frequently. Add more water as needed to prevent liquid from cooking away.*

*Taste for seasoning at end of cooking time. If a spicier chili is desired, add additional chili powder to taste. If more seasoning is added, cook an additional 30 minutes to allow spices to cook in.*

# FIREBARN CHILI

## SERVES 8 TO 10

INGREDIENTS

2 tablespoons (30 g) lard or bacon drippings

1 large onion, coarsely chopped

3 pounds (1⅓ kg) very lean beef, such as chuck tender, coarsely ground

2 medium cloves garlic, finely chopped

1 can (8 ounces/225 g) tomato sauce

1 tablespoon ground hot red chile peppers (cayenne or serrano)

1 tablespoon ground mild red chile peppers (California or New Mexico)

¼ cup (35 g) chili powder

2 teaspoons ground cumin

1½ teaspoons salt

# JOHN BILLY CHILI

## SERVES 10 TO 12

### INGREDIENTS

2 tablespoons fat rendered from
chopped beef kidney suet or
same amount vegetable oil

4 pounds (1¾ kg) beef chuck tender,
cut into chunks the size
of sugar cubes

1 medium onion, finely chopped

4 large cloves garlic, peeled

1 tablespoon garlic salt

½ tablespoon monosodium glutamate
(MSG), divided (optional)

1½ teaspoons salt, divided

¾ cup (175 mL) or more beef
bouillon or broth

1 can (8 ounces/225 g) tomato sauce

¼ cup (35 g) chili powder

1 heaping tablespoon ground ancho
chile, or 1 large dried ancho chile,
softened and peeled (see note)

2 tablespoons ground cumin

1 tablespoon paprika

White pepper to taste, approximately
1 to 1½ tablespoons

1 large or 2 small jalapeño peppers,
halved, seeded and stemmed

*John Billy Murray's 1984 Original Terlingua International Frank X. Tolbert–Wick Fowler Memorial Championship Chili.*

*In large, stainless-steel pot, render enough fat from suet to make approximately 2 tablespoons. Remove suet and discard. Add beef cubes and cook over high heat until meat turns gray.*

*To meat, add onion, whole, peeled garlic cloves, garlic salt, ¼ tablespoon MSG, ¾ teaspoon salt, and bouillon. Cover and cook over medium heat at rapid boil about 45 minutes or until meat is tender. The meat should be tender enough to squeeze flat between your fingers without bouncing back.*

When meat is tender, reduce heat. Add tomato sauce, cover, and simmer 15 minutes. If desired, remove garlic cloves or mash and incorporate into chili. Add remaining MSG and salt, chili powder, ancho chile, cumin, paprika, white pepper, and jalapeño halves.

Cover and simmer an additional 45 minutes, stirring frequently. Add additional broth (or liquid from softened ancho) very sparingly as needed during remaining cooking time, to prevent meat from cooking dry. At end of cooking time, remove jalapeños and discard.

Chili should be a thick consistency so that a 10-inch wooden spoon will stand upright in the chili, then slowly sink to the bottom.

## Note

*To soften dried ancho chile: Seed and stem the pod and place under a broiler to blacken the skin. Soak blackened chile in warm water for 10 to 15 minutes: scrape pulp from skin and discard skin. Use softened chile as indicated.*

Opposite: Chili Tostada Stack (p. 83)

# BEYOND THE BOWL

# CHILI ON THE HALF SHELL

## SERVES 4 TO 8

INGREDIENTS

4 large baking potatoes
¼ cup (60 g) butter, melted
Salt and pepper to taste
1½ cups (350 mL) homemade chili
or 1 can (15 ounces/425 g) chili,
heated
1 cup (115 g) grated cheddar cheese
½ cup (125 mL) sour cream
3 green onions, chopped,
including tops

*Preheat oven to 400°F (200°C). Scrub potatoes and prick with a fork to allow steam to escape. Bake 1 to 1¼ hours or until potatoes respond to pressure when squeezed with a pot holder. If desired, potatoes may be cooked in microwave according to manufacturer's directions.*

*Preheat broiler. Halve baked potatoes and scoop out inside of potatoes, leaving ¼-inch (¾-cm) thickness on skins. Reserve pulp for other uses. Cut skins in half again and brush with melted butter. Season to taste with salt and pepper.*

*Place under broiler and cook until edges brown, 3 to 5 minutes. Pour heated chili over potato skins. Garnish with cheese, sour cream, and chopped onion. Makes 4 main dish servings, or 8 appetizer servings.*

Sauté onion and garlic in oil in large saucepan 5 minutes or until onions are translucent. Add tomatoes and green chilies and puréed tomatoes along with chicken stock, chili powder, cumin, and salt. Cover and simmer 45 minutes.

Meanwhile, fry tortilla strips in small amount of oil in a skillet just until barely crisp. Drain on paper towels.

Just before serving, add tortilla strips and cooked chicken, if desired, to soup. Cook 5 to 10 minutes longer. Serve garnished with a sprinkling of diced avocado, cheese and a dollop of sour cream.

# HINT OF CHILI TORTILLA SOUP

## SERVES 6 TO 8

INGREDIENTS

1 onion, chopped
2 cloves garlic, minced
1 tablespoon vegetable oil
1 can (10½ ounces/300 g) tomatoes with green chilies, undrained and chopped
1 can (14½ to 16 ounces/450 g) puréed tomatoes
3 cups (700 mL) chicken stock
1 teaspoon chili powder
1 teaspoon ground cumin
Salt to taste
4 corn tortillas, cut into ¼ × 1½-inch (¾ × 4-cm) strips
1 cup (175 g) diced, cooked chicken, if desired
Diced avocado
Grated cheddar or Monterey Jack cheese
Sour cream

# CHILI CORNBREAD

## SERVES 8 TO 10

INGREDIENTS

2 eggs, beaten
1½ cups (350 mL) thick homemade chili or 1 can (15 ounces/425 g) chili
1 cup (240 mL) sour cream
1 medium onion, finely chopped
½ cup (70 g) flour
2 cups (340 g) yellow cornmeal
1 teaspoon baking soda
1 teaspoon salt
1½ cups (175 g) grated Monterey Jack cheese with jalapeños

*Combine eggs, chili, sour cream, and onion in small bowl; set aside. Combine flour, cornmeal, baking soda, and salt in large bowl. Pour liquid ingredients into dry mixture all at once. Quickly stir, just to moisten cornmeal. Gently fold in cheese.*

*Preheat oven to 375°F (190°C). Grease a 10-inch (25-cm) cast-iron skillet or 9-inch (23-cm) square pan. Warm pan in oven to melt shortening. Bake 35 to 40 minutes or until top is golden and center is firm. Cut into wedges or squares and serve immediately.*

Combine butter and oil in a large, shallow baking pan, such as a jelly roll pan. Place in a 300°F (150°C) oven just long enough to melt butter.

Remove from oven, add red pepper sauce, and mix well. Add peanuts and toss to coat evenly. Spread nuts in single layer and bake for 30 minutes, stirring occasionally.

Combine chili powder, paprika, and salt. Remove nuts from oven after 30 minutes. Sprinkle nuts with seasonings and toss well to coat on all sides. Return to oven and bake for 15 more minutes. Allow to cool and drain on paper towels.

## Variation

**CHILI PUMPKIN SEEDS** *Scrape seeds from large pumpkin, rinse well to remove pumpkin "strings," and drain on paper towels. Proceed as with peanuts. Bake until crisp and dry.*

# CHILI PEANUTS

### MAKES 1 POUND

INGREDIENTS

2 tablespoons (30 g) butter
2 tablespoons vegetable oil
1 to 2 teaspoons red pepper sauce
1 pound (450 g) raw peanuts, shelled
4 teaspoons chili powder
1 teaspoon paprika
2 teaspoons salt

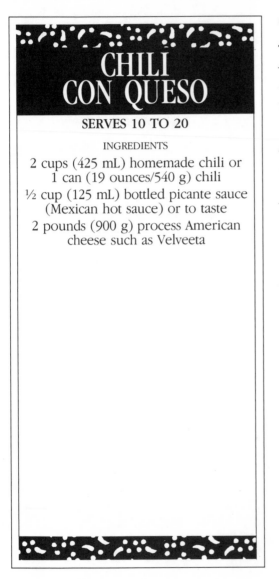

# CHILI CON QUESO

**SERVES 10 TO 20**

INGREDIENTS

2 cups (425 mL) homemade chili or
1 can (19 ounces/540 g) chili

½ cup (125 mL) bottled picante sauce
(Mexican hot sauce) or to taste

2 pounds (900 g) process American
cheese such as Velveeta

*Gently heat chili and picante sauce in large saucepan. Meanwhile, cut cheese into large cubes. When chili is warm, stir in cubed cheese. Continue heating over low heat, stirring frequently, until cheese is melted.*

*Adjust seasoning by adding more hot sauce if a spicier dip is desired. If mixture is too thick, add a bit more hot sauce or milk.*

*Serve in chafing dish or crockpot with plenty of corn or tortilla chips for dipping. (Recipe may be heated in crockpot or chafing dish, if time allows.)*

*Preheat oven to 325°F
(160°C). Spread tortilla chips
in single layer in jelly roll
pan or ovenproof serving
dish. Spoon chili over chips.
Sprinkle cheese, then
jalapeño slices, evenly over
chips. Place in oven until
cheese melts, 5 to 10 minutes.*

*Quickly dollop chips with
guacamole and sour cream.
Sprinkle with tomato. Serve
warm. Makes 6 to 8 appetizer
servings or 4 main dish
servings.*

## Note

**GUACAMOLE** *Peel, seed, and mash
1 large ripe avocado in small bowl.
Stir in 1 tablespoon lemon or lime
juice, salt to taste and ¼ teaspoon
garlic powder. Add a dash of red
pepper sauce, if desired. Makes
approximately 1 cup (240 mL).*

# CHILI NACHOS

### SERVES 4 TO 8

INGREDIENTS

1 small bag (approximately 7 ounces/
200 g) tortilla chips

1½ cups (350 mL) homemade chili
or 1 can (15 ounces/425 g) chili,
heated

1½ cups (175 g) grated
cheddar cheese

¼ to ½ cup (30-60 g) sliced,
pickled jalapeño peppers

1 cup (240 mL) guacamole,
approximately (recipe below)

1 cup (240 mL) sour cream

1 tomato, finely chopped

# CHILI TACOS

## SERVES 4 TO 5

INGREDIENTS

1 can (16 ounces/450 g) refried beans
8 to 10 crispy taco shells
1½ cups (350 mL) homemade chili
or 1 can (15 ounces/425 g) chili
1 small onion, chopped
2 cups (175 g) shredded lettuce
1 tomato, chopped
1 cup (115 g) grated cheddar cheese
Picante sauce, if desired

*Spread refried beans in taco shells. Place taco shells upright in baking pan in 325°F (160°C) oven for 10 minutes to crisp and heat through.*

*Meanwhile, heat chili in saucepan. When taco shells are hot, spoon hot chili over beans in tacos. Top with onion, lettuce, tomato and cheese.*

*Serve with picante sauce to taste.*

Opposite: Five-Way Cincinnati Chili (p. 50)

Preheat oven to 350°F (180°C). Lightly grease or spray with non-stick spray a 1½-quart (1½-L) casserole or 10-inch (25-cm) cake pan.

Spread a small amount of chili in bottom. Place a tortilla over chili and spread with beans. Sprinkle beans with some of onions, then pour a layer of chili over onions. Sprinkle with some of cheese. Repeat layers—tortilla, beans, onion, chili, and cheese—until all ingredients are used, ending with chili and cheese.

Bake for 25 to 30 minutes, or until chili bubbles and cheese is melted. Let set 5 minutes before cutting into wedges.

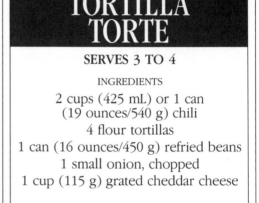

# CHILI TORTILLA TORTE

## SERVES 3 TO 4

INGREDIENTS

2 cups (425 mL) or 1 can (19 ounces/540 g) chili
4 flour tortillas
1 can (16 ounces/450 g) refried beans
1 small onion, chopped
1 cup (115 g) grated cheddar cheese

# CHILI BURRITOS

**SERVES 3 TO 6**

INGREDIENTS

6 flour tortillas

1½ cups (350 mL) homemade chili or 1 can (15 ounces/425 g) chili, heated

¾ cup (85 g) grated cheddar or Monterey Jack cheese

1 cup (85 g) shredded lettuce

1 small tomato, chopped and drained

Sour cream

Salsa verde (Mexican green sauce) to taste, approximately ¼ cup (60 mL)

*Wrap flour tortillas tightly in foil and place in 350°F (180°C) oven 10 to 15 minutes to warm. Meanwhile, heat chili in saucepan. When tortillas are warm, soft, and pliable, place ¼ cup (60 mL) hot chili in center of each.*

*Top with a sprinkling of cheese, shredded lettuce, and diced tomato. Roll tortilla and place seam side down on warm plate. Reserve and keep warm. Repeat with remaining tortillas, chili, lettuce, and tomato.*

*Garnish each burrito with a dollop of sour cream and salsa verde. Sprinkle with additional cheese if desired. Makes 6 burritos.*

Preheat oven to 350°F (180°C). Heat chili and refried beans separately in small saucepans. Meanwhile, season mashed avocado to taste with salt, picante sauce and lemon or lime juice. Place the seed in the mashed avocado to prevent darkening and reserve.

Fry tortillas on both sides in ½ inch (1½ cm) oil in large skillet until crisp; drain on paper towels. If using packaged tostada shells, omit this step.

Spread 6 crisp tostada shells with refried beans and arrange in an ovenproof serving dish or on a baking sheet. Spoon chili over beans. Spread remaining tostadas with beans, then place on top of filled shells on baking sheet. Spoon chili over tostada stacks and sprinkle with cheese.

Bake for 5 to 10 minutes. Garnish each stack with lettuce, tomato, and dollops of avocado and sour cream. Spoon additional picante sauce and chopped cilantro over each, if desired.

# CHILI TOSTADA STACK

## SERVES 6

### INGREDIENTS

1½ cups (350 mL) homemade chili or 1 can (15 ounces/425 g) chili
1 can (16 ounces/450 g) refried beans
1 large avocado, peeled, seeded and mashed, reserve seed
Salt to taste
1 tablespoon picante sauce, or to taste
1 teaspoon lemon or lime juice
12 soft corn tortillas or packaged crisp tostada shells
1½ cups (175 g) grated cheddar or Monterey Jack cheese
Shredded iceberg lettuce
Chopped tomato
Sour cream
Chopped fresh cilantro, if desired

# CHILI-MAC

## SERVES 6 TO 8

INGREDIENTS

2 pounds (900 g) lean ground beef
1 medium onion, chopped
2 cloves garlic, minced
3 tablespoons chili powder
1 teaspoon salt
1 tablespoon ground cumin
1 can (14½ to 16 ounces/450 g)
tomatoes, undrained and chopped
1 can (8 ounces/225 g) tomato sauce
1 cup (115 g) uncooked elbow
macaroni
1 can (15 ounces/425 g) pinto beans,
undrained

*Cook beef and onion in large skillet over medium-high heat until beef loses color and onion is soft, about 5 minutes. Drain excess fat. Sprinkle with garlic, chili powder, salt, and cumin. Stir to coat meat well.*

*Add tomatoes and tomato sauce; stir. Cover and simmer over low heat 15 minutes. Add macaroni, cover, and continue cooking 15 minutes or until macaroni is tender. Add beans and heat through.*

## Variation

**SCARY CHILI** *Serve Chili-Mac in a pumpkin for Halloween. Cut top off pumpkin to form a lid. Scoop out membrane and seeds. Rinse and reserve seeds to roast, if desired. (See variation of Chili Peanuts recipe.) Rinse pumpkin well, inside and out; drain. Decorate outside of pumpkin with markers for a Jack-o-lantern effect. While Chili-Mac is cooking, place pumpkin on ovenproof serving platter and heat in 300°F (150°C) oven 10 to 15 minutes. Pour hot chili mixture into warm pumpkin and serve.*

Preheat oven to 325°F (160°C). Combine rice and sour cream in bowl. Spread half the rice mixture in the bottom of a 1½-quart (1½-L) casserole which has been lightly greased or sprayed with non-stick spray.

Spread 1 cup (240 mL) chili over rice. Sprinkle with onion, then half of cheese. Repeat layers of rice, chili, and cheese.

Place in oven and heat until bubbly around the edges, approximately 20 to 30 minutes.

# CHILI RICE CASSEROLE

## SERVES 4 TO 6

INGREDIENTS

2 cups (175 g) cooked rice
2 cups (425 mL) sour cream
2 cups (425 mL) homemade chili or
1 can (19 ounces/540 g) chili, divided
1 small onion, finely chopped
2 cups (225 g) grated mild cheddar
or Monterey Jack cheese, divided

# FRITO CHILI PIE

## SERVES 4 TO 6

### INGREDIENTS

2 cups (425 mL) homemade chili
or 1 can (19 ounces/540 g) chili
1 large onion, chopped
2 cups (225 g) grated cheddar
or Monterey Jack cheese
4 cups (510 g) crushed corn chips

*Frito Chili Pie is a popular family-style dish that probably dates to the convenience era in food, the late 1950s to the 1960s when food manufacturers were doing their best to help housewives spend less time in the kitchen. It was popularized with Frito brand corn chips, before the introduction of tortilla chips. Hence the name. This dish is one of the few that begs for canned chili. It evolved into an even more convenient dish when someone discovered that the easiest way to make a Frito Chili Pie was to slit open the side of a small bag of corn chips and pour chili inside the bag. This version is called Walk-Away Chili Pie. Frito Chili Pie enjoyed a renaissance when it was the hit of the 1982 World's Fair in Knoxville, Tennessee.*

*Preheat oven to 325°F (160°C). Place 1 cup (240 mL) chili in bottom of 1½-quart (1½-L) casserole dish which has been lightly greased or sprayed with nonstick spray. Layer with half of the onion, half the cheese and half the chips. Repeat layers, ending with chips. Place in oven for 30 minutes or until bubbly. Remove from oven and let stand 10 minutes before serving.*

# CHILI HASH BROWNS

**SERVES 4**

INGREDIENTS

2 to 3 tablespoons vegetable oil
1 pound (450 g) frozen hash browns
(½ package)
1 small onion, chopped
Salt and pepper to taste
1 can (4 ounces/115 g) seeded and
chopped green chiles, drained
1½ cups (350 mL) homemade chili
or 1 can (15 ounces/425 g) chili
½ cup (60 g) grated cheddar or
Monterey Jack cheese

*Preheat a 10-inch (25-cm) skillet. Add oil. Spread potatoes and onion evenly in bottom of ovenproof skillet and cook according to package directions. Season to taste with salt and pepper.*

*When potatoes are brown and crusty, remove skillet from heat. Sprinkle green chiles over potatoes, then pour chili evenly over potatoes. Sprinkle with cheese and place in 350°F (180°C) oven 20 to 30 minutes or until chili is heated through.*

Opposite: Chili Hash Browns

Cut tortillas into bite-size pieces. In large skillet, fry in 1/4 inch (3/4 cm) of hot oil until crisp; drain on paper towel. Pour all but 1 to 2 tablespoons oil from skillet and add onion. Sauté until onion is soft.

Lower heat to medium low and add a tablespoon or so of butter to skillet, if desired. Pour eggs into skillet and add tortilla chips and salt and pepper. Stir eggs gently.

When eggs are almost set, pour chili over eggs and stir gently. Cook until eggs are set and chili is heated through. Remove skillet from heat and sprinkle cheese over eggs. Cover skillet with lid to melt cheese. If desired, sprinkle fresh tomato over eggs. Serve hot with warm flour tortillas.

# MIGAS CON CHILI (SCRAMBLED EGGS WITH CHILI).

**SERVES 3 TO 4**

INGREDIENTS

5 corn tortillas
Vegetable oil
1 small onion, chopped
Butter
6 eggs, beaten
Salt and pepper to taste
1/2 cup (125 mL) chili
1/2 cup (60 g) grated cheddar cheese
Chopped tomato (optional)

# CHILI QUICHE

## SERVES 6 TO 8

### INGREDIENTS

½ cup (115 g) grated Monterey Jack cheese
¼ cup (60 g) grated cheddar cheese
1 teaspoon flour
1 10-inch (25-cm) chili pastry crust (see recipe) or prepared pastry shell
½ pound (225 g) ground beef
1 medium onion, chopped
1 tablespoon chili powder
1 teaspoon ground cumin
1 tablespoon tomato paste or ketchup
3 eggs, beaten
1½ cups (350 mL) milk
¼ teaspoon ground nutmeg
½ teaspoon salt
⅛ teaspoon pepper
Dash of cayenne pepper
2 tablespoons chopped fresh cilantro

*Preheat oven to 400°F (200°C). Combine cheeses and toss with flour to coat well and separate strands. Sprinkle cheese in bottom of prepared pastry shell.*

*Sauté meat in large skillet. Add onions and sauté until meat loses color and onions are soft, about 5 minutes. Drain excess fat. Stir in chili powder, cumin, and tomato paste or ketchup. Spread meat mixture over cheese.*

*Beat together eggs, milk, nutmeg, salt, and peppers in bowl. Stir in cilantro. Pour over meat and cheese. Place quiche dish on baking sheet and bake 15 minutes; reduce heat to 325°F (160°C) and bake for 20 minutes or until custard is set. Cool 10 minutes before cutting into wedges. Serve warm.*

## *Note*

**CHILI PASTRY**  *Combine 1 cup (140 g) unbleached flour, 2 teaspoons chili powder, 1/2 teaspoon salt and 1/4 teaspoon garlic powder. Cut 1/3 cup (85 g) shortening into flour. Gradually stir in 1/4 to 1/3 cup (60-75 mL) cold water to make a stiff dough. Shape dough into a flat disc and refrigerate 30 minutes to 1 hour for easier handling. Roll out on a lightly floured board and place in a 10-inch (25-cm) pie pan or quiche pan with removable sides. Trim edges and flute, if desired. Bake at 350°F (180°C) for 10 minutes.*

# CHILI AND CHEESE SOUFFLÉ

## SERVES 4

INGREDIENTS

3 tablespoons (40 g) butter
2 tablespoons flour
½ teaspoon salt
½ teaspoon dry mustard
¼ teaspoon paprika
1 cup (240 mL) evaporated milk
½ cup (60 g) grated cheddar cheese
1 cup (240 mL) homemade or
canned chili
3 eggs, separated

*Preheat oven to 350°F (180°C). Grease a 1½-quart (1½-L) soufflé dish. Melt butter in saucepan. Add flour, salt, mustard, and paprika; stir until smooth. Gradually add milk. Cook and stir over medium heat until thickened. Add cheese and chili, remove from heat, and stir until cheese is melted.*

*In small bowl, beat 3 egg yolks. Stir in a small amount of cheese mixture. Slowly pour egg mixture back into cheese and chili mixture, stirring briskly.*

*Beat egg whites until stiff peaks form. Fold chili and cheese mixture carefully into egg whites. Pour into prepared soufflé dish and bake for 35 to 40 minutes until soufflé is puffed and golden.*

In a large skillet, sauté onion and garlic in oil until soft. Add tomatoes, mushrooms, green chiles, zucchini, chili powder, salt, oregano, cumin, and black pepper. Simmer, covered, until vegetables are tender, about 15 minutes.

Combine flour with water to make a smooth paste. Add to vegetables, along with beans. Cook and stir until thickened, about 5 minutes. Serve over hot, cooked rice. Sprinkle with shredded cheddar or Monterey Jack cheese, if desired.

# ZUCCHINI AND TOMATO CHILI WITH RICE

## SERVES 4 TO 6

INGREDIENTS

1 onion, chopped
2 cloves garlic, minced
2 tablespoons vegetable oil
2 cans (14 to 16 ounces/425-450 g) whole tomatoes, chopped
3 cups (340 g) sliced fresh mushrooms
1 can (4 ounces/115 g) chopped green chiles
2 cups (225 g) sliced zucchini (½-inch/2½-cm)
1 tablespoon chili powder
1¼ teaspoons salt
1 teaspoon crushed oregano leaves
½ teaspoon ground cumin
⅛ teaspoon ground black pepper
1½ tablespoons flour
3 tablespoons water
1 can (8¾ ounces/250 g) pinto beans, drained
2 cups (340 g) hot cooked rice

# STUFFED MANICOTTI WITH CHILI

## SERVES 3 TO 4

### INGREDIENTS

1½ cups (450 g) ricotta
½ cup (2 ounces/60 g) shredded
Monterey Jack cheese with jalapeños
1 egg, lightly beaten
2 tablespons chopped fresh cilantro
⅛ teaspoon salt
Dash of pepper
6 manicotti shells, cooked, drained,
and rinsed
1½ cups (350 mL) homemade chili
or 1 can (15 ounces/425 g) chili

*Preheat oven to 350°F (180°C). Grease a 9-inch (23-cm) baking dish.*

*Combine ricotta, ¼ cup (30 g) shredded Monterey Jack cheese, egg, cilantro, salt, and pepper. Stuff manicotti shells with cheese mixture. Place shells in baking dish. Spread chili evenly over stuffed manicotti and sprinkle chili with remaining shredded cheese. Bake for 25 minutes or until heated through.*

## Note

*You can substitute plain Monterey Jack cheese for the cheese with jalapeños.*

This is a mild, hamburger chili which is good for entertaining large groups. Guests can spice it up with a variety of condiments as they would curry, hence the name.

Cook ground meat, onion, and green pepper in a large skillet or pot until the vegetables are soft and the meat loses color. Drain off fat. Add tomato sauce, beans, Worcestershire sauce, chili powder, red pepper sauce, and salt to taste. Cover and simmer for about 1 hour, stirring occasionally.

Serve chili in bowls with the following condiments and accompaniments allowing guests to customize their chili:

Chopped black olives
Cubed avocado, sprinkled with lemon juice and lightly dusted with cayenne, if desired
Grated cheddar and Monterey Jack cheeses
Shredded lettuce
Mexican hot sauce (salsa)
Tortilla chips
Cooked rice
Chopped onion
Cooked noodles or macaroni

# JOANNE EVERTS' TEXAS CURRY

## SERVES 4

INGREDIENTS

1 pound (450 g) ground beef chuck
1 onion, chopped
1 green pepper, seeded and chopped
1 can (15 ounces/425 g) tomato sauce
1 can (23 ounces/650 g)
chili-flavored beans
1 tablespoon Worcestershire sauce
2 tablespoons chili powder
Dash of red pepper sauce
Salt to taste

# PICADILLO WITH MEXICAN CHILE RICE

## SERVES 6

### INGREDIENTS

1 pound (450 g) ground beef or
½ pound (225 g) ground beef and
½ pound (225 g) ground venison
1 onion, chopped
2 cloves garlic, minced
1 can (14 to 16 ounces/425–450 g)
tomatoes, chopped but undrained
¼ cup (60 mL) dry red wine
or dry sherry
Water
1 teaspoon salt
⅛ teaspoon pepper
¼ cup (30 g) raisins (optional)

*Cook the meat in a skillet over high heat until meat loses color, crumbling meat with the back of a spoon. Add onion and garlic; cook until onion is soft.*

*Combine tomatoes and their liquid, wine, and enough water to make 2 cups (450 ml). Add to meat mixture along with salt and pepper. Bring liquid to a boil, reduce heat, cover, and simmer 15 minutes.*

*Remove cover, add raisins if desired, and cook an additional 15 minutes longer or until meat is tender and some of the liquid is cooked away and thickened. Serve over Mexican Chile Rice (recipe follows).*

Heat oil in a saucepan over medium heat. Add rice and cook until rice is opaque. Stirring frequently, add onion and cook until onions are wilted and rice begins to brown. Add salt, warm broth, cumin, and chili powder. Bring liquid to a boil, reduce heat, cover, and simmer until rice is tender and liquid is absorbed, 14 to 16 minutes.

Remove lid, fluff rice, and stir in drained peas.

# MEXICAN CHILE RICE

**SERVES 6**

INGREDIENTS

3 tablespoons vegetable oil or bacon drippings
1 cup (225 g) raw rice
½ teaspoon salt
1 onion, chopped
2 cups (450 mL) beef broth, heated
1 teaspoon ground cumin
1 tablespoon chili powder
1 can (8½ ounces/240 g) tiny green peas, drained

# INDEX

# FAVORITE RECIPES

# FAVORITE RECIPES

# FAVORITE RECIPES

# FAVORITE RECIPES

---

---

---

---

---

---

---

---

---

---

*With special thanks to Tom and Kelly for tireless tasting, to Prissy for tireless testing, and to Carol and the Gang for sharing their knowledge of chili.*

## ACKNOWLEDGMENTS

The author is grateful to the following sources for allowing her to reprint their chili recipes in this book:

Hammond Incorporated, Maplewood, New Jersey, for the Texas Chuckwagon Chili, from the *Food Editors' Hometown Favorites Cookbook*.

International Chili Society, for Carroll Shelby's Chili, Fred Drexel's 1981 Winning Recipe, Bill Pfeiffer's 1982 World Championship Chili, Harold R. Timber's 1983 World Championship Chili, and Dusty Hudspeth's 1984 Championship Chili. Reprinted from *The Official International Chili Society Cookbook*. "World Championship Chili Cookoff"® is a registered service mark of the International Chili Society.

Richardson's Woman's Club, for Frank Tolbert's Chili Recipe, from *The Texas Experience*. Courtesy of the Richardson Woman's Club.

The author is also grateful to the following individuals for allowing her to use their recipes in this book: Paul Brian (1983 Terlingua Winner), Bill "Ice-T" Douglas (Hurricane Billy's Chili), Joanne Everts (Texas Curry), Rock V. Grundman and Scott Nickson (Deep Hole Chili), John Billy Murray (John Billy Chili), Nancy Parker (Texas Gourmet Chili), Bo Pilgrim (Chicken Chili), Amber Robinson (Big Mama's Oklahoma Chili), Tom Skipper (Ol' Blue Chili), David Talbot, Jr. (Silver Bullet Chili), and Steve Weaver (Firebarn Chili).

Dotty Griffith is an award-winning food writer and editor with more than ten years' newspaper experience. She has been food editor of the weekly section of the *Dallas Morning News* for the past five years, and has served as a judge for several national cooking contests, has been a regular guest host for the food section of a cable television show, and has served on the nutrition task force of the American Heart Association. She brings her enthusiasm for all types of food—but especially chili—to this new book in the Barron's series.